Contents

	Introduction	2
1	Overriding a Spook	3
2	Outsmarting a Jigger	7
3	Stopping a Grass Snatcher	13
4	Longeing for Respect—Preparation	17
5	Longeing for Respect—Circling	21
6	Longeing for Respect—Changing Directions	25
7	Suppling on the Trail	29
8	Desensitizing to Traffic	33
9	Crossing Water	37
10	Gaining Your Horse's Respect	41

About the Authors

CLINTON ANDERSON
Clinton, the only two-time winner of the Road to the Horse colt-starting challenge, is one of the top clinicians in the world today. His down-to-earth, common-sensical training methods have proven popular with horse owners of all types. His weekly training series is the most-watched equine program on RFD-TV, and his book, *Downunder Horsemanship*, is a best-seller. "Training on the Trail," the *Horse & Rider* series from which this program is adapted, was the 2004 first-place winner in American Horse Publications competition. Clinton and his wife, Beth, reside at their state-of-the-art training facility in Belle Center, Ohio. The native Australian regularly travels around the country, presenting horsemanship clinics and headlining at horse expos. For more information, go to www.clintonanderson.net.

JENNIFER FORSBERG MEYER
Jennifer, an award-winning journalist and author, is an editor-at-large with *Horse & Rider* magazine. In addition to producing feature articles, special reports, and training pieces, she pens a monthly column, "The Riding Family." The author of two books, she's also writer/editor of *Growing Up With Horses: A Parent's Handbook & Resource Guide*, a Primedia/*Horse & Rider* annual publication. A lifelong horsewoman, she lives in Northern California with her husband and their pony-enthusiast daughter, Sophie Elene.

Introduction

If you love to ride on the trail, you've probably run into problems at one time or another—jigging, spooking, balking at water, and others described in this program. I ran into them, too, when I was a horse-crazy kid in my native Australia. I needed answers.

To find them, I became a "clinic junkie." I went to as many educational sessions as I could. At first, horsemanship seemed magical and confusing. Clinicians would say, "just do this," but I'd discover it didn't work quite the same way when you tried it on your own. So I'd go back and ask more questions, then go home and work out the details with my own and the neighborhood kids' horses.

Gradually, horse training began to seem less like magic and more like common sense.

I refined my methods later, while starting colts and fixing problem horses for a living, when I did a large part of my training out on the trail. Then, when I came to America in the mid-1990s and began giving clinics myself, I tried my methods with all kinds of horses across the U.S.—and found that they worked.

The core of my approach is to command a horse's respect by moving his feet, which activates the thinking side of his brain. This approach also "turns negatives into positives." That's because you take a wayward horse's energy and use it to teach him something useful—instead of fighting with him.

In this program, I'll show you how my methods provide practical solutions to trail-riding problems. Lessons 1 through 3 explain how to cure spooking, jigging, and grass-snatching. In Lessons 4 through 6, you'll learn my method of "longeing for respect," a great tool for activating your horse's thinking brain and tuning him in to you.

Lesson 7 explains how to use time on the trail to supple your horse, and Lessons 8 and 9 will teach you how to remove his fear of traffic and of water. Lesson 10 is a summary of my training philosophy, which is all about gaining your horse's respect.

Here and there throughout this program are sprinkled questions from readers who were following the lessons when they first appeared as a monthly series in *Horse & Rider*. My answers to their real-world dilemmas will help you better understand the rationale behind my methods.

So apply my solutions to your horse's trail-related problems, and you can head out for that ride with "no worries," mate!

—*Clinton Anderson*

LESSON ONE

USE THESE TECHNIQUES TO REMAKE YOUR HORSE INTO AN ENJOYABLE, RELIABLE TRAIL COMPANION.

When something frightens your horse, don't stop and face the object. Instead, move your horse around it to get him thinking rather than reacting.

1 Overriding a Spook

ONE | Overriding a Spook

EVERYONE LOVES A TRAIL RIDE. IT'S ONE OF THE MOST relaxing, pleasurable things you can do with your horse. But what about when it's not relaxing? What about when your horse is spooky, jigging, tossing his head, or otherwise refusing to move along willingly?

I can help you there, mate. In my clinics across the country, I get more questions regarding trail-riding problems than almost anything else. That's made me work hard to come up with solutions that will work for most riders, and with most horses. Before I became a clinician, I worked on a ranch in Australia, my native land, where I handled literally hundreds of unbroke or spoiled horses. I did much of my training out on the trail, rather than in an arena. As a result, I don't think there's a trail-related problem I haven't run into—and figured out how to fix.

In this program, I'll share my methods for dealing with the most common problems you'll face on the trail. I'll show you how to use your horse's wayward energy—when he's spooking, jigging, or otherwise acting up—to correct his behavior and teach him something useful. I'll also cover some of the most common pilot errors—things you may be doing to set your horse up for failure on the trail. Finally, I'll show you how to use the trail to supple your horse and make him lighter and more responsive for any kind of riding.

In this first lesson, I'll teach you what to do when your horse spooks. In the past, you may have dealt with this problem by stopping and facing the "scary" object, while attempting to persuade your horse that it won't hurt him. Though this approach may eventually calm him down, it probably won't keep him from spooking at the same object again, the next time he sees it.

By contrast, my approach is to keep a horse's feet moving when he spooks. It's more effective (I'll explain why in a moment) and safer than letting your horse stop and tense up. Plus, it helps you stay calm and focused, by giving you something to do other than react to your horse's fear. And one other bonus—while you're training your horse not to spook, you're also suppling him and teaching him how to use his feet in a turn.

I'll show you how to circle around the offending object, changing directions every one-and-a-half revolutions. This approach—constant movement and turning—overrides your horse's natural instincts. It pulls him out of the reactive side of his brain (the part that shouts: "Don't stop and think—RUN! Or you'll be KILLED!"), and moves him into the thinking part. This occurs because the repeated turning requires him to think about maneuvering his feet, which otherwise will get tangled up.

At the same time, this method teaches your horse that spooking is a no-win proposition for him. In essence, you're saying, "Okay, you want to spook? Then let's *hustle*." It's classic reverse psychology; eventually your horse says, "Hey—I don't want to 'spook' anymore!" He's learned "spook" translates into "work" rather than a nice break with stroking and kind words.

If you use my method consistently, your horse will eventually decide to give up spooking as a strategy and instead concentrate on being your willing partner (because it's less work). As you've probably noticed, horses are inherently lazy—they dream about sleeping. So if you make his way hard work and your way a breeze, he'll soon be going your way.

Sound good? Then let's get to it.

BEFORE YOU HEAD OUT…

…for this lesson or any of the future lessons in this program:

■ Be sure your horse is broke enough to be out on the trail. If he's lacking basic stop, go, and turn controls, then what you need isn't trail training, but help from my other, more basic training materials (www.clintonanderson.net). As an alternative, have a reputable trainer work directly with your horse until the necessary basic skills are in place.

■ Make sure you'll be in the right company. If you choose to do your training during a group ride, the other riders must support your training goals and be willing to wait for you if need be while you school your horse. In any event, the total number in your group should be no more than three or four; any larger will be overly distracting to your horse.

■ Check that the weather is appropriate. Don't go out on windy and/or frigid days, which can make your horse too rambunctious from the get-go. The trail you choose should have reasonably safe footing—this isn't the time for steep, rocky, slippery, or otherwise treacherous terrain.

■ Do groundwork first. You want your horse in the right frame of mind—that is, paying attention and respecting your requests—before you even mount up. If he's not respecting you on the ground, he surely won't respect you when you're mounted. So longe him, work him in the round pen, or do whatever you ordinarily do to dissipate his excess energy, assess how he's feeling, and get him tuned in to you.

■ Give him time to settle in once you do hit the trail, and then *ride every step of the way*. Don't be gabbing with your friends or gazing at the scenery. There will be time for that later, in moderation. Right now, give your full attention to your horse and how he's responding—or not—to your cues.

1. When your horse spooks on the trail, get his legs moving immediately. I've placed a red box in my path to give my mare something to spook at. But instead of letting her stop and face the "scary" object, I move her into a circle around it. This puts me back in control, and takes my mare's heightened energy and does something positive with it. To move your horse in a counter-clockwise circle as I am here, apply light pressure on your left rein (carrying that hand a bit to the left if need be) to tip your horse's head in the direction of the circle. At the same time, apply left-leg pressure at the cinch and right-leg pressure behind it to encourage brisk forward movement—at least a trot—and a slight bend on the circle. By requiring your horse to move around the object—rather than letting him stop and face it—you're engaging the thinking side of his brain, thus overriding the fear response coming from his reactive side.

IF YOU CAN'T CIRCLE THE SPOOK OBJECT...

...then simply make a circle as near it as you can. If, for example, what's frightening your horse is a rock outcropping on the side of a steep hill next to where you're riding, move your horse in an active circle as close to the outcropping as he'll allow. If you have to begin with a 15-foot circle 15 feet away from the outcropping, that's okay. Every time you approach the rocks, reverse your direction by turning your horse toward the outcropping (thus to the outside of your circle), making your horse's feet hustle. Continue on in this manner until you can bring the circle closer to the outcropping, and your horse relaxes and accepts approaching the rocks in return for going slower and eventually stopping.

2. After you've traveled one-and-a-half times around the object, reverse direction by turning your horse in toward the object. To do this, sit deep in your saddle and carry your inside rein (in this case, your left rein) back toward your inside hip to bring his head around. At the same time, apply outside- (right-) leg pressure at the cinch or just in front of it to further encourage your horse's front end to roll back to the left. Then continue to circle the object in the opposite

ONE Overriding a Spook

direction, moving your horse at a speed that's just a little faster than he wants to go. This is an exercise that can't be done at a walk. You need vigorous movement to take command of your horse, tire him, and take the "fun" out of spooking. Continue on like this, turning in toward the object after every one-and-a-half revolutions.

3. As your horse becomes more and more focused on the turning and circling—and less nervous about the object—you'll be able to bring him closer to it, as I am here. Do this by applying outside-leg pressure just behind the cinch and gentle pressure on the inside rein. If you're unable to make as small a circle as I am here, that's okay. Make the circle as large as it needs to be to find your horse's comfort zone, and then push him on, gradually decreasing the size of the circle over time.

4. As you continue, your horse will increasingly regard you as his leader—because you're calling all the shots on what he does with his feet. This will increase his confidence and further lessen his fear of the object. You'll feel his body relax, and he'll stop looking at the object so intently. At this point, allow your horse to lessen his speed and move more slowly around it, as I am with my mare, here.

5. After your horse is relaxed enough to come down to a quiet walk, test his acceptance by using your inside rein to tip his nose directly toward the object. If he's relaxed and willing to do so, as my mare is here, your mission is accomplished. If he tenses up, send him on for another few revolutions and turns.

6. Eventually, this will be your horse's response—happy to stand still, even if it means being nearly on top of the object! Now's the time to stroke and praise him—while he's truly relaxed and accepting the object, rather than while he's fearful of and resisting it. ■

LESSON TWO

TRAIN THE JIGGING AND HEAD TOSSING OUT OF YOUR TRAIL HORSE WITH THIS TAKE-CHARGE APPROACH.

Does your horse refuse to walk on the trail, preferring to bounce along in that irritating, uncomfortable walk-prance known as a jig? Pulling on the reins won't make him stop—you've already discovered that. But you can train him out of this behavior with this horse-smart approach.

2 Outsmarting a Jigger

TWO — Outsmarting a Jigger

IN LESSON 1, YOU LEARNED HOW TO HELP OVERRIDE YOUR horse's spook response by keeping his feet moving, thus activating the thinking—rather than reacting—side of his brain. In this lesson, you'll use a similar strategy to convince your horse that jigging and head-tossing on the trail just aren't worth the effort.

Jigging—that mincing, half-prance horses fall into when they want to establish the pace and you won't let them—is a symptom of nervousness. (It may also indicate a lack of a proper foundation, something I'll discuss further under "To Get The Most From This Lesson.") If nervousness at being in unfamiliar surroundings is the cause of your horse's jigging, you can help him overcome his jitters by putting his feet to work making circles. This obliges him to use the thinking side of his brain and reasserts your control of the situation (because you are determining in which direction those feet go).

It also puts his excess energy to good use, and convinces him that attempting to jig is not worth the resulting effort demanded of him. Eventually, he'll come to view flat-footed walking on a loose rein as a much-needed vacation. And that's right where you want him to be.

The key to my approach is preparing your horse properly before you ever hit the trail, and then using one rein rather than two when he does try to jig. When you take up on both reins in an attempt to stop your horse's jigging, you're simply inviting resistance, and a head-toss. Your horse's response in this situation is similar to that of a racehorse: The more the jockey pulls on the reins, the faster the horse wants to go. Plus, when your horse is already nervous, pressure on both reins feels claustrophobic to him, further activating his get-away response.

Instead, you're going to use one rein to bend your horse into a tight circle and keep him on it for four or five revolutions, or until he begins to relax and slow down to a walk of his own accord. Then you'll circle the other way, further relaxing and suppling him, and prompting him to use his thinking brain. You'll repeat this procedure whenever he tries to jig, until he decides he just doesn't want to "go there" anymore.

SAFETY FIRST

If, at any point during this lesson, you feel unsafe in the saddle, dismount and resume the groundwork described in Photo #1. After 10 to 20 minutes of "longeing for respect," if you're still not sure you can control your horse from the saddle, that's a clear sign that he's lacking foundation basics. Return home—on foot if need be—and follow the advice set forth in the second bulleted item, below.

TO GET THE MOST FROM THIS LESSON:

- Review the "Before You Head Out" caveats on page 4.
- Determine whether your horse is jigging because he lacks a solid foundation in the basics. He is if he won't respond willingly to your cues to walk, jog, and lope quietly both ways of the arena, changing direction and stopping without a fuss. If this describes your horse, then you need arena time, not a trail ride. Seek out a reputable trainer or take other measures to make sure basic skills are in place before you go out on the trail. (There are many tools to help you, including those on my website, **www.clintonanderson.net**.)
- Jigging is only worsened by the presence of other horses, so avoid groups while you conduct your training sessions. Ideally, ride with just one sensible companion mounted on a quiet, seasoned trail horse.
- Select terrain with wide, flat expanses, rather than narrow or confined trails. You'll need plenty of room to move your horse in circles and trot on when needed.
- If a mecate rein isn't part of your bridle, carry a halter and a lead rope that's at least 14 feet long in case groundwork is needed out on the trail.
- Don't expect to cure your horse of jigging in just one lesson. Ideally, schedule short sessions several times a week, for as many weeks as necessary. (The definition of "short" will depend on your horse. In general, keep going until he begins to feel at least a little more relaxed than when you started. Quit there, and then build from that during your next ride.) And don't even consider adding more than one companion to your rides until your horse has been walking quietly for several sessions.

1. Before you head out to the trail, relax and supple your horse—and get the "fresh" out so he'll tune in to you—with some groundwork basics. I use a technique I call "longeing for respect," which involves sending your horse around you at a brisk trot, asking for a change of direction every two or three circles. The difference between my method and more traditional longeing is twofold: First, the focus is on those brisk changes of direction, which activate a horse's thinking brain. Second, I want some slack in the line, which indicates a horse's responsiveness and respect. I create this slack by pulling and releasing the line in a way that tells my horse, "If you stay light and responsive to my body language, I'll stay light and won't drag on your face." Once your horse is warmed up, supple, and focusing exclusively on you (which should take no more than 10 to 20 minutes of longeing, or perhaps a bit more, depending on how fresh your horse is), you're ready to head out.

2. Now, if your horse still wants to jig when you get out on the trail, here's what not to do: pull back on both reins. When you do this, your horse will either do what mine is here—tuck behind the vertical to avoid bit pressure—or toss his head. Pulling is actually what causes a jig: Your horse is nervous and wants to move ahead at his own pace, but your hands aren't letting him, so he settles for a half-walk, half-trot—a jig. Pulling like this will not stop your horse from jigging.

TWO Outsmarting a Jigger

3. Instead, the moment you feel your horse get jiggy, take him up on his offer to move forward by letting him commit to a full trot, rather than a tentative jig. Say, "OK, if you want to go, let's go!" and let him trot on for 10 feet or so.

4. Then, decide which direction—left or right—will give you the best space for circling, and slide the hand on that side down the rein to prepare to ask for a seven- to eight-foot-diameter circle in that direction. By doing this, rather than resisting your horse's impulse to "go," you're saying, "Thank you very much for taking off. Now, let's do some circles to get light and supple." Note that I'm sliding my hand a fair bit down the rein—at least eight to ten inches. Plus, note the slight slack in the other rein, because I do not want pressure on both sides of my mare's mouth.

5. Follow through with a pull-and-release pressure on the rein that's initiating the circle. Your hand should move back toward your hip—the place where the seam of your jeans meets your belt—then release back toward your knee as your horse begins to respond. Then ask again. As you ask with your rein, also apply pressure at the cinch with the leg on the same side, to arc your horse's body around your leg (as you move into the circle, this will be your inside rein, inside leg). That's what I'm doing here, and my mare is beginning to initiate a tight turn to the right. Again, note the slack in the opposite rein, which gives her the latitude to turn her head, and keeps her focus on the inside rein.

Here's what it looks like when I do it the wrong way. I'm asking for a circle to the left, but I'm pulling on my right rein, as well, instead of allowing it to stay slack. My mare is beginning to turn, but she's resisting my double-fisted approach by bowing her neck (your horse might also toss his head). I'm sending her a mixed message: turn, don't turn! Note the difference in her expression here and in Photo #5. Here, she's feeling overly confined. In #5, she's focused on the turn.

10 CLINTON ANDERSON TRAINING ON THE TRAIL

6. Don't be bashful about asking your horse to bring his head right around toward your toe as you ask for this small circle. Your goal, again, is to get him soft, supple, and responsive to you. Your horse likely will not be as supple as mine is here the first few times you ask for the circle, and that's OK. Do the best you can, and gradually make the circle smaller as you pull and release, and your horse begins to loosen up. In general, the more bend you can get, the better. Continue on like this for four or five revolutions, or until your horse begins to relax. You'll know he's relaxing when you feel less tension on your rein hand, and he drops his head and neck, and slows his trot. Then circle in the other direction for four or five revolutions. If your horse is volunteering to walk at that point, go ahead and send him straight on with a loose rein (or at least ultra-light contact), in essence daring him to jig. If he does, simply repeat the circling/suppling a couple more times, then ask again for a flat-footed walk.

HOME, NOT-SO-SWEET HOME

If your horse jigs mainly when he's headed home, he's probably anticipating the pleasant things that happen when he arrives: You get off his back, remove the saddle, brush his itchy spots, and turn him out—or put him back in his cushy stall—to relax and doze. You may even feed him, too, so what red-blooded horse wouldn't be eager to get home?

To change his attitude about "headin' back"—and thereby make it easier to implement your no-jigging strategies on the return trip—change the routine once you get home. Rather than putting your horse up, continue to ride him for 20 or 30 minutes. Make it a genuine work session, too, with plenty of vigorous trotting, loping, and changes of direction.

Then, once you've cooled him out, let him stand safely tied for a couple of hours to remind him about patience.

Finally, if possible, don't feed him until a bit later, so there's no chance he associates getting home with getting fed.

If you follow this routine several times in a row, and then periodically from then on, your horse will stop anticipating his homecoming with such eagerness, and you'll have a better chance of training away his jigging.

7. If your horse still doesn't want to walk after 20 minutes of off-and-on circling, send him on at a brisk trot everywhere you go. Zig-zag down the trail, go up and down slight hills and rises, or ride large circles, figure eights, and serpentines in a clearing. Mix it up—but keep that forward energy going. He'll eventually tire, and take you up on an offer to walk. Then, if he starts jigging again later, resume the circling/suppling and, if necessary, the trotting on until he's ready to walk again. Over time (and it may take multiple sessions), your horse will opt to skip the jig/circle/trot-on sequence and go straight to walking.

For variety, trot your horse around elements of the terrain, such as bushes and trees. Giving him specific tasks to do while trotting briskly keeps his mind engaged—and on you—while he works off his jigginess. ■

CLINTON ANDERSON TRAINING ON THE TRAIL **11**

TWO Outsmarting a Jigger

MAKE EVERY MOMENT COUNT

If you're like most amateur horse owners, you have to work to find time to fit all your horse activities—not just your trail rides—into an already-busy day. Here are my tips for making the most of every moment you spend with your horse each week.

- **Cluster your training days.** If you have only three days a week to ride, you'll accomplish more in your training if you can make those days consecutive, rather than spread throughout the week. This is especially true when you're attempting to teach your horse something new. Horses need consistent, repeated training sessions until a learned response becomes a habit. After that, they can go longer periods of time and still retain their training.

  For example, when my horses get the weekend off, I find they have "Monday-itis" when I begin riding again at the start of the week. I have to go back and repeat what I was teaching them on Friday, because they've lost most of it. On Tuesday, I can pretty much pick right up from where we left off on Monday. On Wednesday, we progress from Tuesday, and so on. That way, I make actual progress in all but the first of the days I ride that week.

  If, by contrast, you ride, say, on Monday, Wednesday, and Saturday, you're dealing with "Monday-itis" every time you ride, so your horse progresses much more slowly.

The old horseman's adage is absolutely true: You're either training— or untraining—your horse every moment you're with him.

- **Train all the time.** By this I mean, require some sort of obedience from your horse every moment you're with him. When you're cleaning his stall, have him move around you, rather than vice versa. If he puts his head up when you're putting his blanket on or taking it off, pause a moment to desensitize him to the blanket and remind him to remain still. As you're leading him, insist that he follow obediently, without hanging back or dragging you forward.

  The old horseman's adage is absolutely true: You're either training—or untraining—your horse every moment you're with him.

- **Mind the small stuff.** Your horse is constantly reading you in an effort to determine, "Is he/she serious, or not?" He'll test you in small ways—push into your space, wait a heartbeat before responding to your request, attempt to "get an inch" here and there—then observe how you respond. If you don't correct him on these small "cheats," he'll eventually pull a much larger one.

  At that point, you may feel he's acting "out of the blue." But, in reality, he's been telling you for some time, via those little cheats, that he's losing respect for you. Problem is, you haven't been "listening"—or correcting him.

  —*Clinton*

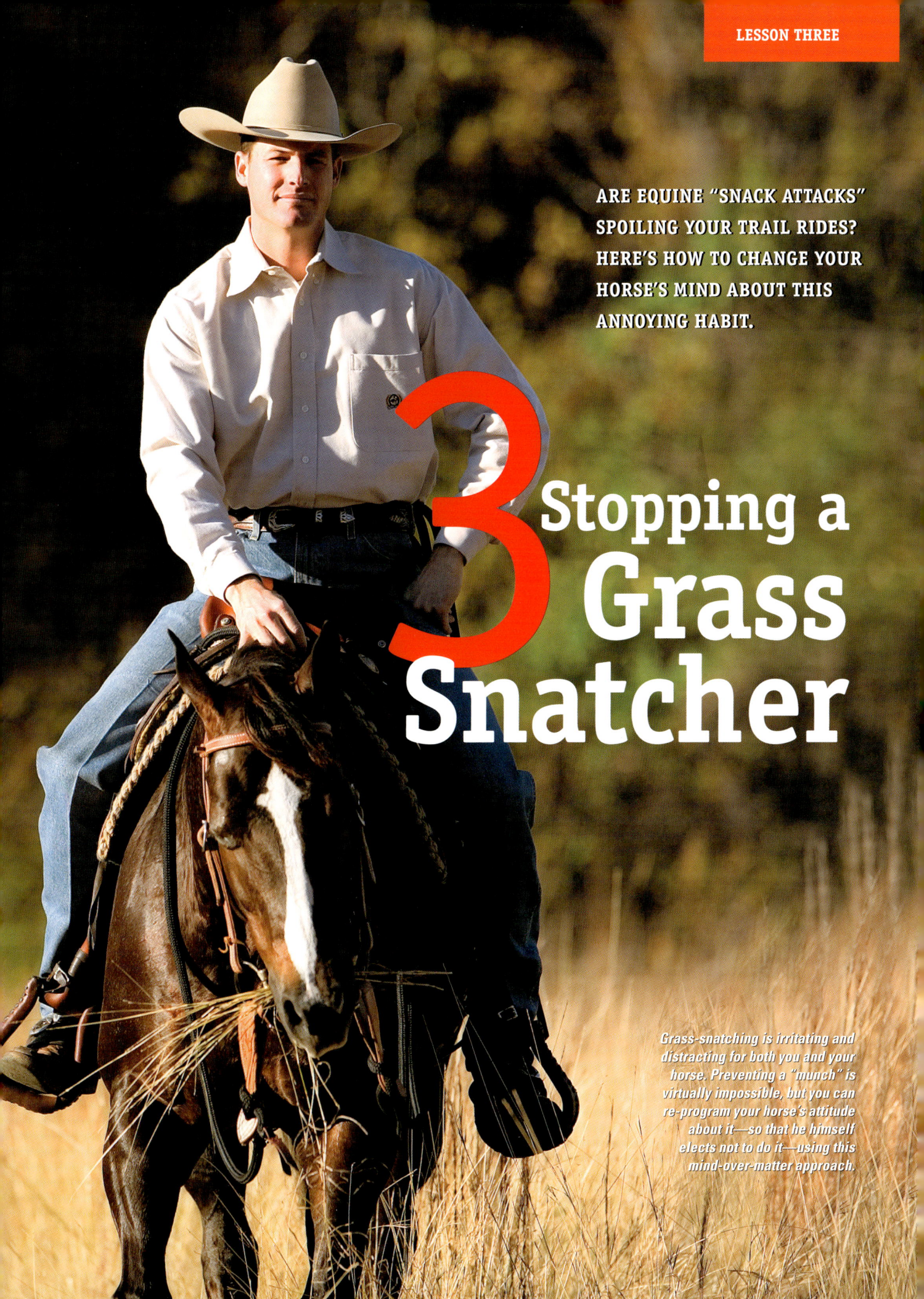

LESSON THREE

ARE EQUINE "SNACK ATTACKS" SPOILING YOUR TRAIL RIDES? HERE'S HOW TO CHANGE YOUR HORSE'S MIND ABOUT THIS ANNOYING HABIT.

3 Stopping a Grass Snatcher

Grass-snatching is irritating and distracting for both you and your horse. Preventing a "munch" is virtually impossible, but you can re-program your horse's attitude about it—so that he himself elects not to do it—using this mind-over-matter approach.

THREE Stopping a Grass Snatcher

BY NOW, YOUR TRAIL HORSE IS LOSING HIS PENCHANT FOR spooking (Lesson 1) and jigging (Lesson 2). You've changed his behavior by teaching him that such naughtiness only brings him more work. Now it's time to use the same strategy to convince him that grass-snatching isn't a good idea, either.

Munching on scenery is the ploy of a food-obsessed horse that doesn't have enough to think about. The typical muncher is not a big troublemaker, he just loves to eat. Strolling down the trail gives him the opportunity to think about—and act upon—his desire. Horses have one-track minds. If they're truly focused on what you're asking of them, they tend not to get into mischief. But too often riders engage in what I call the "recipe trail ride"—ambling down the trail, swapping recipes. When you leave your horse to his own devices like this, you open the door to grass-snatching.

People generally think prevention is the key. They ask, "How can I keep my horse from snatching at grass?" I tell them this is the wrong approach. Instead, they must re-program their horse's attitude about munching by letting him do it—then making him pay the price. That price is serious exertion—circles, serpentines, side-passes, and other exercises that cause him to move his feet, change direction, and work hard.

How does this work? Think of your favorite pizza, or any food you find irresistible. Now, imagine trying to eat it while you're running at a brisk trot and continuously changing direction. You wouldn't be able to enjoy that pizza, would you? Well, neither can your horse enjoy his stolen mouthful when you're making him think and work hard.

With repetition, eventually a light will turn on in his head. "Hmmm...every time I open my mouth, I get *awfully* busy." This is *not* a desirable option, especially for a lazy horse—the stereotypical grass-snatcher. Thus, over time, he learns to forego the bite to avoid the work. It's mind over munching.

(And, there's a bonus: As you're teaching your horse to eschew chomping, you're also schooling him to be more supple and responsive overall. It's a win-win proposition.)

1. As you ride in areas where your horse will be tempted to grab a bite, give him every opportunity to take the bait. Remember, you're not keeping him from munching, you're letting him do it, but taking the pleasure out of it so he gives it up of his own accord. So, the instant he *does* wrap his lips around a mouthful...

TO GET THE MOST FROM THIS LESSON:

■ Review the "Before You Head Out" caveats in Lesson 1 on page 4.
■ Don't take your horse out when he's famished, but do arrange to ride when his appetite will tempt him at least a little.
■ Select terrain with wide, flat expanses, rather than narrow or confined trails. You'll need plenty of room to move your horse around when needed.

■ Don't expect to cure your horse of grass-snatching in just one lesson. Ideally, schedule training rides several times a week, for as many weeks as necessary. Remember, training is as important for a trail horse as it is for a show horse. You don't expect a show horse to automatically know what you want, or to "get it" in just one or two lessons. Take the time necessary to turn your horse into a well-schooled trail companion.

2. ...put him right to work. In this case, I'm asking for a sidepass to my right by tipping my mare's head to the left with my left rein, and applying left-leg pressure just behind the cinch to ask her to step laterally to the right (note her hind leg stepping under her belly). After you've taken a few sidepass steps to the right...

3. ...reverse these cues to sidepass your horse to the left. Go back and forth a few times—making him work!—then resume your ride. Sidepassing isn't as energetic as some of the other exercises we'll do, but because it involves lateral movement, horses do find it demanding, so it still serves nicely as negative reinforcement for grass-snatching.

BE CONSISTENT!

If you want your "no-eating" message to stick, don't do what I'm doing here—allowing my horse to graze at a rest stop. Horses are professional cheats—give them one exception, and they'll finagle their way to others. If you let your horse graze while he's standing still, he'll eventually want to do it at other times, too, and you'll have sabotaged your retraining program.

At a minimum, don't let your horse eat anytime he's bridled, whether you're mounted or not. My personal preference is to forbid eating whenever I'm with my horse. From the moment I slip that halter on, I want my horse's attention on me—and nothing else.

This kind of consistency actually makes a horse's life easier all the way around.

FINDS 'CHANGES' CHALLENGING

Dear Clinton,
I tried the "longeing for respect" as you described it in the lesson, "Outsmarting a Jigger", but found the frequent changes of direction quite demanding for both me and my horse. Is this really an essential part of the method?
– *Julia Adamson, Bellevue, Iowa*

Dear Julia,
Yes, and in fact it's *the* essential part. These changes of direction activate the thinking part of your horse's brain, which in turn enables him to pay attention and learn. They also increase your horse's respect for you, because by making him change direction, you're controlling the movement of all four of his feet—both his forehand and hindquarters. In my version of longeing, you also command respect by insisting that your horse remain light in your hand. Your ultimate goal is to accomplish the longeing with slack in the line. You encourage this lightness with a pull-and-release approach—pulling on the line whenever he pulls against you, using only as much pressure as necessary to get him to lighten. Then, you reward him by pitching him slack the instant you feel less pressure on the line.

I'll explain all this in greater detail next lesson, when we'll focus on longeing for respect.
–*Clinton*

THREE Stopping a Grass Snatcher

4. The next time your horse swipes a bite, try a small (say, seven- to eight-foot-diameter) circle to the left. Do this by sliding your left hand eight to 10 inches down the rein, then taking that hand back toward your hip (or, as I like to say, the place where the seam of your jeans meets your belt), as I am here, in a pull-and-release pressure. Leave slack in your right rein to allow your horse's head to come around, and apply pressure at the cinch with your left leg, to arc your horse's body around that leg. Move your horse briskly, and after two or three revolutions…

5. …reverse these cues for a few small circles to the right. Repeat the circles in each direction, then let your horse move off down the trail again, allowing him to relax until he tries to grab another bite.

6. When he does snatch again, if the terrain allows, move him forward at an extended trot for 50 feet, then bend him onto a circle, then trot on for 50 feet, and then circle again, for two or three cycles. This combination of brisk trotting and repeated bending and turning is particularly demanding. You can vary the pattern to make it interesting, too—ride serpentines, zig-zag up and down rises, or even circle around some bushes or trees. Don't work your horse until he's dripping sweat—that's overdoing it. But push him hard enough to establish the connection in his mind between illegal eating and exertion. With time, he'll give up the one to avoid the other. ■

LESSON FOUR

DOES YOUR TRAIL HORSE NEED A "TIME OUT?" USE THESE UNIQUE LONGEING TECHNIQUES TO REFOCUS YOUR HORSE'S ATTENTION—AND HONE HIS CAN-DO KEENNESS. THIS LESSON: LONGEING PREP.

4 Longeing for respect—Preparation

When difficulties arise, fighting with your trail horse isn't the answer. Instead, strengthen the bond between the two of you and sharpen your horse's willingness with the groundwork sequence I call "longeing for respect."

FOUR   Longeing for Respect—Preparation

IF YOU'VE FOLLOWED MY LESSONS SO FAR, YOU'RE learning to avoid fighting with your horse. When he does something you don't want, such as spooking or jigging, you take the energy he's created and redirect his feet to teach him something positive (e.g., how to be supple and more responsive). In the process, you kill his appetite for the wrong behavior.

Sometimes, though, if your horse is being particularly resistant, you may need a "time out" to relax him and sharpen his respectfulness. By controlling his feet in a series of turns that I call "longeing for respect," you activate the thinking side of his brain and remind him how he's supposed to respond to you: with lightness and willingness.

You can longe for respect before you head out on the trail (in fact, I recommend it), and you can carry a 14-foot lead with you (if you don't have a mecate rein) so you can repeat the exercise, if needed, during your ride. The respect and lightness you foster through longeing will carry over when you remount and ride on.

In this lesson, I'll teach you the in-hand exercises that prepare your horse for my form of longeing. These exercises include desensitizing him to training tools, disengaging his hindquarters, disengaging his forequarters, and backing. In Lesson 5, you'll learn how to use these in-hand skills to send your horse onto the longeing circle, and then have him stop and face you. In Lesson 6, you'll complete the sequence by learning how to direct your horse in smooth, continuous, repeated turns on the hindquarters while on a circle.

TO GET THE MOST FROM THIS LESSON:

- Outfit your horse in a rope halter with a lead that's at least 14 feet long. I prefer my own halters, which have extra knots on the noseband for improved responsiveness, but any of the stiffer rope halters will do. If you don't have a training stick, you can make one of your own (using a sturdy, four-foot-long stick with a six-foot-long detachable rope string), or else use a dressage whip.
- Take the necessary time to teach your horse these maneuvers. Short training sessions every day (say, for 20 to 30 minutes) are preferable to longer, less frequent ones. If you can train only three days a week, make them consecutive days, to enable your horse to build on the prior day's lesson.

1. First, desensitize your horse to your training tools. Take the lead rope and rub it all over him. Start gently, and then use a firmer pressure as you proceed. Cover every part of his body, including under his belly and down his legs.

2. Next, desensitize him further by repeatedly flinging the rope over him and pulling it back to you in a smooth, steady rhythm. Swing the rope over and/or around every body part, including his legs. Work from both sides of his body. (Repeat this desensitizing periodically, even after you've advanced in the longeing lesson. That way, even though you'll be using your lead and other training tools to drive and correct your horse, he won't come to fear them.)

3. Now, desensitize your horse to the training stick or whip by gently moving it all over both sides of his body. Once he's OK with that, flick the string or the end of the whip around his legs.

5. The disengagement is complete when your horse is looking at you with both eyes, as my gelding is here. When that happens, gently rub your horse's forehead with your stick or whip. (Repeat this gentle rubbing anytime you've used the stick to motivate your horse, and he's responded properly. Again, you don't want him to fear your training tools, or you.) Once he'll move his hindquarters consistently in one direction, step to his other side and repeat the process to disengage his hindquarters in the opposite direction.

4. When your horse is completely comfortable with the lead and stick or whip, teach him to disengage his hindquarters—that is, to step his hind end laterally away from you. Do this by crouching slightly and looking intently at your horse's hindquarters as you step toward them, as if to step on his tail. If necessary, tap him on the hindquarters with your stick or whip to encourage him to step to the side, away from you, with his hind legs. (Tap lightly at first. If he doesn't respond, increase the intensity until he does.)

6. Now, use your stick and your rope hand to encourage your horse to disengage his forequarters—that is, to step laterally away from you with his front legs, pivoting on his hind end. Stand next to your horse's head, hold your rope hand up by his eye, as I am here, and with your other hand tap lightly on his neck with the stick, increasing the intensity of the taps until he steps aside. Once he'll move his forequarters consistently in one direction, step to his other side and repeat the process to disengage his forequarters in the opposite direction.

CLINTON ANDERSON   TRAINING ON THE TRAIL   19

FOUR Longeing for Respect—Preparation

7

7. Now, repeat Step 4 (disengaging the hindquarters) and, once your horse is facing you, immediately ask him to back up, as I'm doing here, by gesturing "back" with your hands and using the forcefulness of your intent to "push" him back. If necessary, in the beginning you also can shake the lead shank and/or tap his chest with the stick until he gets the idea. The goal is to combine the two movements into one flowing maneuver, such that your horse steps his hindquarters to the side and then immediately backs up. When he'll consistently perform the maneuver in one direction, step to his other side and repeat the process. ■

HORSE JIGS ON WOODED TRAILS

Dear Clinton,
My 20-year-old Arabian gelding gets excited and jigs only on wooded trails, where there's no room to make circles (Lesson 2, page 8). He's wonderful in open spaces and on wider, "groomed" trails, but hates feeling closed in. What can I do to help him?

Susie Faver,
Hamilton, Ontario, Canada

Dear Susie,
Find a trail that has at least a little bit of room on it. You don't need to be able to execute a full circle, but you do need to channel his energy in some constructive way. When he starts jigging, try zigzagging at a brisk trot, weaving in and around some trees, or even trotting up and back one segment of the trail. This will eventually cause him to associate jigging with hard work. What you want to avoid is going directly from riding in one extreme (open spaces) to the other (narrow, confined trails). That will heighten his feelings of claustrophobia. Try to find a progression of trails to ride on, from open to gradually more closed in.

—Clinton

LESSON FIVE

WHEN YOUR TRAIL HORSE IS RESISTANT, TAKE A "TIME OUT" TO RELAX HIM AND SHARPEN HIS RESPECTFULNESS, USING MY UNIQUE LONGEING TECHNIQUES.

5 Longeing for respect— Circling

In the second part of our longeing for respect sequence, you'll learn to send your horse out onto a circle, then cue him to turn in, stop, and face you. Controlling the movement of his feet in this manner will strengthen the bond between the two of you and sharpen his obedience.

FIVE Longeing for Respect—Circling

IN THE LAST LESSON, OUR FIRST SEGMENT on longeing for respect, you learned the in-hand exercises that prepare your horse for my form of longeing (you desensitized him to your training tools, taught him to disengage his hindquarters and forequarters, then backed him up).

In this lesson, you'll build on that training to send your horse onto the longeing circle, then have him turn in, stop, and face you. (In Lesson 6, you'll complete the longeing sequence by learning how to direct your horse in smooth, continuous, repeated turns on the hindquarters while on the circle.)

This form of longeing is consistent with my approach to training, which avoids fighting with your horse. Instead, you take the energy he creates in unwanted behavior and use it to teach him something positive. By controlling the movement of his feet in all directions, as you will in my form of longeing, you activate the thinking side of his brain, and reinforce that *you* are in charge of him at all times.

TO GET THE MOST FROM THIS LESSON:

■ Outfit your horse in a rope halter with a lead that's at least 14 feet long. I prefer my own halters, which have extra knots on the noseband for improved responsiveness, but any of the stiffer rope halters will do. If you don't have a training stick, you can make one of your own (using a sturdy, four-foot-long stick with a six-foot detachable string, which will be left off for this lesson), or else use a dressage whip.

■ Take the necessary time to teach your horse these maneuvers. Short training sessions every day (say, for 20 to 30 minutes) are preferable to longer, less frequent sessions. If you can train only three days a week, make them consecutive days, to enable your horse to build on the prior day's lesson.

■ Review with your horse the in-hand exercises from Lesson 4 (desensitizing to tools, disengaging hindquarters and forequarters, backing up) before beginning this lesson.

1. After you've warmed up your horse with Lesson 4's in-hand exercises, send him out on a longeing circle to the left. Stand in front of him, about six feet away from his head. Hold the lead in your left hand, with your knuckles up and your palm facing down. Then, raise that hand, as I'm doing here, to "point" in the direction you want your horse to go. This is always the first step of the longeing sequence.

2. When this doesn't cause your horse to move onto a circle (and most likely it won't, at this point), reinforce the cue with your stick (with string detached—I've tied mine around my horse's neck) or whip. Begin by pointing it toward his head, as I'm doing here. If need be, tap him on the side of his neck to drive him to the left, increasing the intensity of the taps until he responds, much as you did in Lesson 4's disengage-forequarters lesson. If he merely tries to pull away from you, just follow him wherever he goes and keep asking him to move to the left. The moment he does . . .

22 CLINTON ANDERSON TRAINING ON THE TRAIL

3. ... stop tapping and allow him to circle around you. Stay in back of his girth line, as I am here, so that your position drives him onward at a steady trot. (If you position yourself in front of his girth line, your body language is asking him to slow or stop his forward movement.)

4. After three or four revolutions, ask your horse to disengage his hindquarters and turn to face you (this sequence builds upon the disengage-hindquarters sequence from Lesson 4). Pick up the hanging portion of the lead with your right hand (your stick hand), then slide your left hand (knuckles up) down the lead as far as you can reach, as I'm doing here. In the next moment, pull your left hand toward your bellybutton (to draw his head in to face you), step toward your horse's tail with your right leg (as I'm preparing to do here), and swing the stick toward the ground (to drive his hindquarters off the longeing circle).

CLINTON ANDERSON TRAINING ON THE TRAIL **23**

FIVE Longeing for Respect—Circling

5. Once your horse has turned to face you, stopped, and is looking at you with both eyes, as my gelding is here, reward him with a rub on the forehead with the stick. (You want him to regard the stick or whip as an extension of your hand, and nothing to be afraid of.) When he'll respond consistently to Steps 1 through 5, reverse all cues and teach him the same movements going to the right. ■

> ## HORSE PINS EARS DURING GROUND WORK
>
> **Dear Clinton,**
> My 5-year-old Quarter Horse gelding is responding well to your ground work, except for pinning his ears. His attitude isn't ordinarily sour, and he has no apparent lameness or injury that might contribute to this behavior. Despite the ear-pinning, his eyes remain soft and he seems relaxed, although he did make one attempt to bite me. How should I handle this?
>
> – Edward Johnson, Baltimore Maryland
>
> **Dear Edward,**
> Ear-pinning during ground work can be a sign of disrespect, or simply a habit your horse has acquired out of focused effort (like the scowl of an intent tennis player) or boredom. If boredom is the problem, alleviate it by keeping the ground work interesting and fun. Give him reasons to do something—send him over a ground pole or down a gully, or back him up a hill or through water—and don't drill over and over on the same exercise. Attempts to bite are serious offenses and should be dealt with unequivocally: Send your horse onto a vigorous circle or into an energetic back-up, smacking him with your stick if need be to get him to move—*now*. Really hustle his feet—and keep them moving briskly for many moments—so he learns to associate any attempt to bite with instantaneous hard, sustained work.
>
> – Clinton

LESSON SIX

THIS ENERGETIC LONGEING EXERCISE WILL SHARPEN YOUR HORSE'S OBEDIENCE, ENHANCE HIS ATHLETICISM, AND STRENGTHEN THE BOND BETWEEN THE TWO OF YOU.

6 Longeing for respect— Changing Directions

In the final part of our sequence on longeing for respect, you'll learn to direct your horse in a series of smooth, continuous turns on the hindquarters. This exercise activates the thinking side of his brain, improves his balance in rollbacks, and—most importantly—reinforces the message that you're in charge.

SIX
Longeing for Respect—Changing Directions

IN LESSONS 4 AND 5, YOU LEARNED HOW to prepare your horse for longeing, then to send him onto the circle and ask him to stop and face you. In this lesson, in the final segment on longeing for respect, you'll build on that training to guide your horse in a series of smooth, continuous turns on the hindquarters while on the longeing circle.

This form of ground work is great for sharpening your horse's respectfulness. The fast and careful footwork required forces him to think, and because you're controlling his feet as they move in all directions, you're cementing the message that you're in charge of him at all times. As a bonus, this exercise encourages him to collect and work off his hindquarters, thus strengthening him for under-saddle maneuvers.

Longeing for respect is a great pre-ride warm-up. You can also carry a 14-foot lead with you (if you don't already have a mecate rein), so you can repeat the exercise if needed on the trail. The respect and lightness you foster through my longeing techniques will carry over when you remount and ride on.

TO GET THE MOST FROM THIS LESSON:

■ Outfit your horse in a rope halter with a lead that's at least 14 feet long. I prefer my own halters, which have extra knots on the noseband for improved responsiveness, but any of the stiffer rope halters will do. If you don't have a training stick, you can make one of your own (using a sturdy, four-foot-long stick with a six-foot detachable string, which will be taken off for this lesson), or simply use a dressage whip.

■ Take the time necessary to teach your horse these maneuvers. Short training sessions (say, 20 to 30 minutes) every day are preferable to longer ones less frequently. If you can train only three days a week, make them consecutive days, to enable your horse to build on the prior day's lesson.

■ Review with your horse the preparatory in-hand exercises from Lesson 4 and the basic longeing techniques (sending onto the circle; stopping and turning in) from Lesson 5 before beginning this lesson. Don't advance to this exercise until your horse is consistently obedient and respectful in those earlier lessons.

1. After you've warmed up your horse with the in-hand exercises and basic longeing from my last two lessons, send him out on a longeing circle to the left. Make sure he's at least 10 to 12 feet away from you on the circle; if you can touch him with your stick, tap him with it to move him well beyond kicking range. Hold the lead in your left hand, knuckles up, as I am here, and your stick in the other hand. Stay behind your horse's girth line, so that your position drives him forward at a steady trot.

2. To prepare for the stop-and-turn, move the lead to your right hand (knuckles up, thumb pointed toward you) and your stick to your left. Then, step to the left (in front of your horse's girth line) and extend the stick, as I am here, to stop his forward movement. At the same time, raise and "point" with your right hand to indicate the new direction you want him to take. If he learned Lesson 5 well . . .

26 CLINTON ANDERSON TRAINING ON THE TRAIL

3. . . . he'll begin to roll back to change directions on the circle. If he doesn't, keep pointing with your right hand (up at least as high as mine is here), and reinforce the turn request with your stick directed at his neck, as you did in Lesson 4's disengage-forequarters lesson. If he tries to pull away from you, follow him patiently, and keep asking for the turn until he complies ands trots off in the new direction. (If you have extreme difficulty with this step, stop and go back to Lessons 4 and 5 until your horse is confirmed in the stop-turn and send in a new direction.)

4. As your horse responds and moves off in the opposite direction on the circle, encourage him to move briskly, as I am with my body language here. How much encouragement you need will depend on your horse; lazy sorts may need a lot, while hotter types may need none at all.

5. After two or three revolutions in the new direction (more if your horse needs it to become steady), ask for another stop and turn. To prepare, move the rope to your left hand (knuckles up!) and your stick to your right. Then, step in front of his girth line and extend the stick, as I am here, simultaneously raising and "pointing" with your left hand to indicate the new direction you want him to take.

CLINTON ANDERSON TRAINING ON THE TRAIL **27**

SIX | Longeing for Respect—Changing Directions

6. Keep pointing as your horse begins to turn, and keep encouraging him to move energetically with your body language and your stick. As he begins to respond more smoothly and consistently, you can reduce the number of revolutions between turns so that he's moving as little as half a circle before you change directions. This is strenuous work, so keep an eye on your horse's breathing to avoid overworking him. Provide rest stops as needed . . .

7. . . . and plenty of positive reinforcement for good effort. ■

JIGGING HORSE REFUSES TO BEND

Dear Clinton,
My 7-year-old Quarter Horse mare refuses to bend and circle when I try to channel her jiggy energy on the trail. Instead, she goes sideways and tries to get behind the bit so she can take off. I did manage to keep her from running off with me, but I'm a beginner and am finding it difficult to maintain control of her. What should I do?
—Michel Whitney,
Foresthill, California

Dear Michel,
You're not ready to ride this mare on the trail. Go back to basic ground work, including longeing for respect as described in Lessons 4, 5, and 6. When your mare becomes obedient and respectful on the ground, advance to riding her in a confined area, such as a round pen or small arena. Ask her to bend and circle in both directions, and gradually improve her suppleness and willingness before heading back out on the trail. If you run into major problems at any step along the way, seek professional help. As a beginning rider, you should always err on the side of safety when dealing with your horse.

—Clinton

28 CLINTON ANDERSON TRAINING ON THE TRAIL

LESSON SEVEN

7 Suppling on the Trail

A TRAIL RIDE OFFERS A WONDERFUL OPPORTUNITY TO SUPPLE YOUR HORSE. USE THESE EXERCISES TO MAKE HIM SOFTER AND MORE RESPONSIVE ON THE TRAIL *AND* DOWN THE RAIL.

Suppling exercises, such as this move-the-shoulders maneuver, are a terrific way to use your time on the trail to improve your horse.

SEVEN Suppling on the Trail

SO FAR IN THIS SERIES, WE'VE TALKED ABOUT solving trail-riding problems like spooking, jigging, and grass-snatching (Lessons 1 through 3), as well as longeing to sharpen your horse's respectfulness (Lessons 4 though 6). In this lesson, I want to show you how to use trail time as general training time, to make your horse lighter, suppler, and even more responsive, both on the trail and down the rail.

Why train on the trail, instead of in an arena? Because it's effective. I've worked hundreds of colts and problem horses out on the trail, and I find I often get more accomplished there than in an arena. Horses enjoy the work more, as they're less likely to become bored. Like you, they find "going somewhere" more interesting than going round and round in an enclosure.

I'm going to show you how to supple four of your horse's body parts—his head and neck, poll, shoulders, and rib cage—as you ride down the trail. As your horse becomes more flexible and responsive, you'll also be learning how to control each of these body parts—skills that will serve you well in any endeavor, including competition.

> **TO GET THE MOST FROM THIS LESSON:**
>
> ■ As always, be sure your horse is broke enough to be out on the trail in the first place. If he's lacking basic stop, go, and turn controls, stick with round-pen or arena work until the necessary basic skills are in place.
> ■ If you ride with a group (no more than three or four—any more is too distracting), make sure the other riders will be supportive of your training goals.
> ■ Check riding conditions. Frigid or windy days can make your horse too rambunctious, so avoid them. The trail you choose should have reasonably safe footing—nothing steep, rocky, slippery, or otherwise treacherous—and enough open space to work in.
> ■ Before you head out, "longe for respect" (see Lessons 4 through 6) to take the edge off your horse's freshness, assess how he's feeling, and get him tuned in to *you*.

1. After you've "longed for respect" to warm up your horse, head out on the trail and give him time to settle in so that he's walking freely and relaxed, on a loose rein. (If your horse won't go along as nicely as my 2-year-old filly is here, don't worry. The suppling exercises you'll do with him will teach him to value quiet, obedient walking as a pleasant reward.)

30 CLINTON ANDERSON TRAINING ON THE TRAIL

2. To supple your horse's neck to the right, slide your right hand at least eight to 10 inches down the rein, then bring the hand back toward your hip—the place where the seam of your jeans meets your belt. Use a pull-and-release movement—releasing toward your knee—until your horse responds by bringing his head around. Your other rein should remain slack. Once your horse bends his neck fully and brings his head around toward your toe, while walking in a small circle, reverse these cues to bend his neck in the other direction.

3. To supple his poll, squeeze with both your legs as you "hold" with both hands to keep him from simply speeding up. Keep the contact on the reins gentle but insistent until the forward energy you create with your legs causes your horse to flex at the poll and round his topline. The instant he softens, be sure your hands soften as well, to reward him. Suppling his poll will be easier after you've suppled his neck, as lateral flexion smoothes the way for vertical flexion.

4. To supple your horse's shoulders to the right, pick up your left rein to tip his nose to the left, as I am here. At the same time, apply pressure with your left leg at the cinch, to push his shoulders over to the right. (Leg pressure at the cinch moves the shoulders; between the front and back cinches, the rib cage; toward the back cinch, the hindquarters.) Your goal is to have him move from one side of the trail to the other, leading with his shoulders, as my filly is here. Once he does so, reverse these cues to supple his shoulders in the other direction.

CLINTON ANDERSON TRAINING ON THE TRAIL

SEVEN | Suppling on the Trail

5. To supple his rib cage to the left, ask for a sidepass to the left. Holding his neck and shoulders straight with your reins, sit on your right seat bone as I am here and apply right-leg pressure to your horse's rib cage, between the front and back cinches. Keep your left heel away from his side to "open the door" to the left. After he responds with a few steps in that direction, reverse these cues for a sidepass to the right.

6. Between each suppling exercise, and at the conclusion of them, be sure to reward your horse with rubs and kind words, encouraging him to relax as he walks forward with energy. Because simple, straightforward walking is easier than the exercises, he'll begin to view it as a desirable goal—and you'll have a better trail horse. ■

DOMINANT HORSE RUDE TO OTHERS

Dear Clinton,

Your lessons have already helped the jigger, spooker, and grass-snatcher in my family. Now we need help with my son's dominant mare. She has to be at the front of the pack on any trail ride, and pins her ears, kicks out, or even tries to bite if anyone attempts to pass. She's well-behaved in the arena with other horses. Any ideas?
— *Barb Olafsson, Vandalia, Michigan*

Dear Barb,

Whenever your son's mare exhibits this unpleasant behavior, he should redirect her attention and energy toward him and away from the other horse. He achieves this by asking her to do something that requires her to move her feet in various directions; this month's suppling exercises would be perfect. She's got to learn that every time she pins her ears, she's simply saying, "Please train on me." Getting her to realize this will take time and repeated exposure to groups of horses on the trail. Plus, your son must make the work intense enough that she wants to go back to simple walking—which he'll allow only when she agrees to mind her own business.
—*Clinton*

LESSON EIGHT

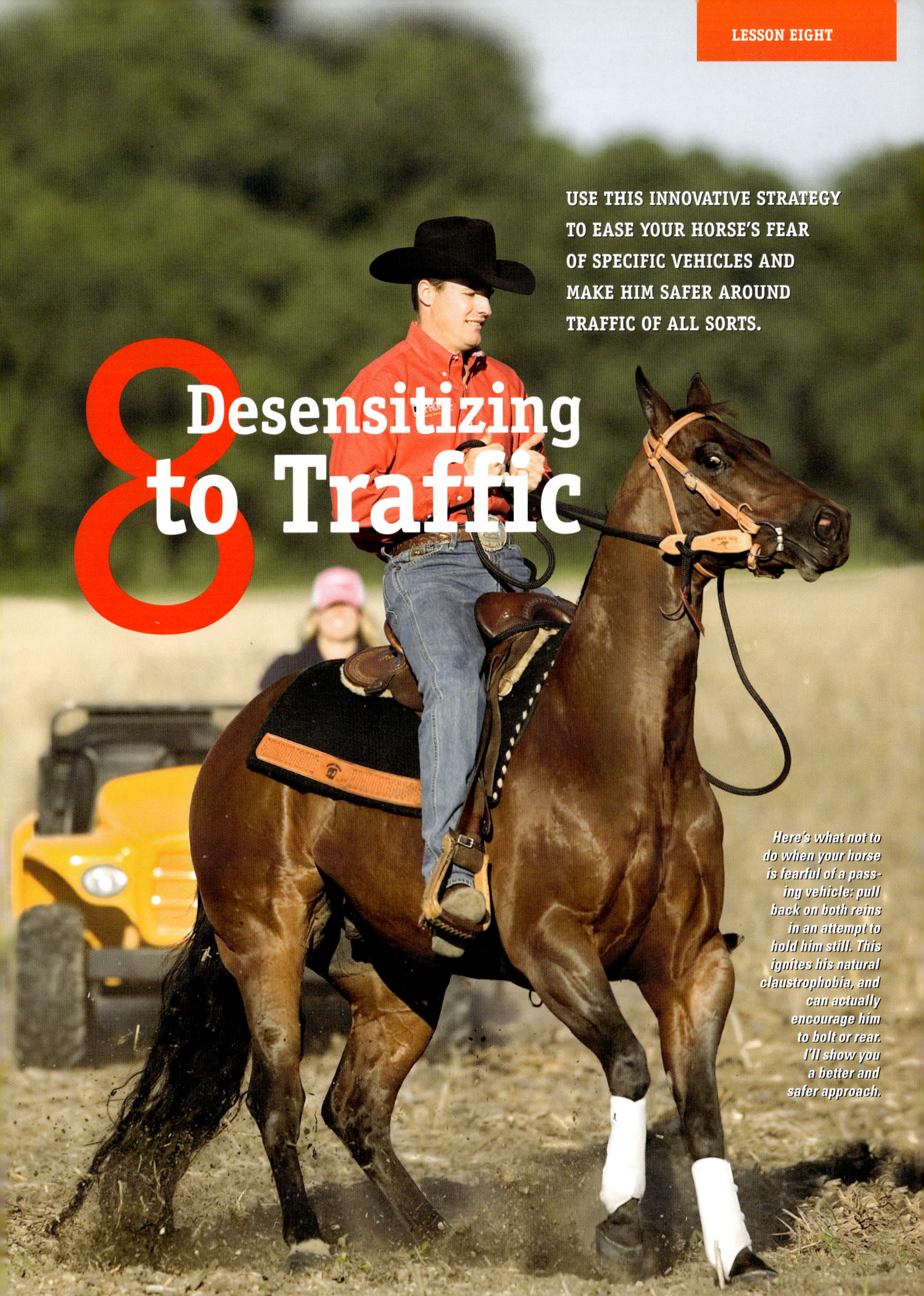

USE THIS INNOVATIVE STRATEGY TO EASE YOUR HORSE'S FEAR OF SPECIFIC VEHICLES AND MAKE HIM SAFER AROUND TRAFFIC OF ALL SORTS.

8 Desensitizing to Traffic

Here's what not to do when your horse is fearful of a passing vehicle: pull back on both reins in an attempt to hold him still. This ignites his natural claustrophobia, and can actually encourage him to bolt or rear. I'll show you a better and safer approach.

EIGHT — Desensitizing to Traffic

IN THIS PROGRAM, I'VE TAUGHT YOU VARIOUS strategies for improving your horse's behavior on the trail, all using the method of moving his feet to engage the thinking side of his brain. Another way to think of my approach is "turning a negative into a positive"—or, turning your horse's naughty energy into exercises that make him lighter and more obedient.

In this lesson, I'll show you how to apply my method to a common problem: fear of vehicles and other moving objects you may encounter when out on a ride. I'll explain why your automatic response—using both reins to hold your horse still—is the wrong approach, and teach you a better way to keep both of you safe while the "scary object" passes.

Then, I'll demonstrate a method you can use at home to desensitize your horse to vehicles and unfamiliar animals by allowing him to "chase" them. Sound strange? Not if you consider the underlying equine psychology.

A horse is somewhat like a dog in the sense that he's much braver when he's chasing something than when he thinks something is chasing him.

Imagine a stray dog barking at you as you walk down the road. If you run away from it, it may well chase after you, barking louder. But if you stop and turn to face it, the dog will stop, and perhaps even retreat a step.

If you then advance menacingly toward the dog, it will almost always turn and run. But if you then stop and begin to retreat again, the dog will begin to advance again. He's what I call a "brave coward."

Your horse is similar. As long as he feels he's being "chased" by something, he's extremely timid and fearful of it. But if he feels *he's* doing the chasing, he becomes emboldened and much less afraid. (Think of a cutting horse's attitude in heading off a cow.)

By setting up practice sessions where your horse can follow after the moving objects that frighten him most, you can desensitize him to those objects. I'll show you how.

1

TO GET THE MOST FROM THIS LESSON:

■ Use common sense. Obviously, if your horse is extremely afraid of vehicles, keep him away from live traffic until you've accomplished the at-home desensitizing, then introduce him to real-life situations gradually. (And, if your horse is lacking basic stop, go, and turn controls, stick with round-pen or arena work and avoid riding out entirely until the necessary basic skills are in place.)

■ If you ride with a group (no more than three or four in total—any more is too distracting), make sure the other horses are calm and secure around traffic and animals.

■ Avoid riding on frigid or windy days, which can make your horse too rambunctious.

■ Before you head out on the trail or attempt the at-home desensitizing, "longe for respect" (see Lessons 4 through 6) to take the edge off your horse, assess how he's feeling, and get him tuned in to *you*.

1. Here and in the photo on the previous page, I'm demonstrating the error most people make when their horse is fearful of a moving object. I'm pulling back on both reins, and attempting to make my horse stand still as the scary object passes. By using both reins to "confine" my horse, I'm making him feel claustrophobic, thus enhancing his fear. This sets him up to bolt or rear—obviously, the exact opposite of the behavior I want.

2. Here's what to do instead. With your horse off to the side of the road, turn him to face the passing object with his chest, and use one rein to flex his head around. This way, he can still see the object, he doesn't feel claustrophobic (because you're not pulling on both reins), and he feels "directed" (rather than simply restrained) by you. Also, if he does attempt to move, he'll be turning in a circle and yielding his hindquarters, and thus is more likely to stay under your control. (If you like, you can use your "other" hand to grab a handful of mane for added security.)

3. Once the vehicle has passed, bend your horse in a few circles each way to get his feet moving. Remember, when you ask his feet to move in various directions, you activate the thinking side of his brain. Your horse then can realize, "Hey—this wasn't so bad, after all."

4. To desensitize your horse to moving objects before you encounter them on a ride, arrange to have the truck, motorcycle, four-wheeler—whatever frightens him—driven slowly while you and your horse follow after it. (If your neighbor's llama is the scary moving object, ask your neighbor to lead the llama while you follow after *it*.) Initially, you won't be able to follow as closely as I am here, and that's OK. Even if you must stay 100 feet back, just continue to follow the vehicle or animal wherever it goes. Eventually, by "chasing" the object like this, your horse will feel less fearful and be willing to move closer to it.

CLINTON ANDERSON TRAINING ON THE TRAIL

EIGHT Desensitizing to Traffic

5. As your horse becomes bolder, have the driver stop and allow your horse to investigate all around the vehicle. Don't force him to do this before he's ready, however; wait until trailing the object has lessened his fear of it. Given time and patient repetition in this way, your horse can be desensitized to about anything that moves, making your trail rides safer and more pleasant. ■

DISRESPECTFUL AT SADDLING

Dear Clinton,

I've done most of your ground work successfully with my mare, but she still stamps her feet and threatens to bite and kick when I try to cinch her up. Why is this, and what should I do?

– Georgia Benyk,
Buckeye, Arizona

Dear Georgia,

A horse can respond well to basic ground work and still have an issue with something specific like cinching up—especially if she's endured rough or hasty cinching by someone in her past. The solution is specific desensitizing. Take your rope and wrap it gently around her heart-girth, as if it were a cinch. If she shows displeasure, ignore her, but keep the rope about her, loosening it the instant she shows the slightest bit of relaxation or acceptance. Do this several times a day for as long as it takes for her to calmly accept the rope's pressure. Then, when you saddle up, take up on the cinch gently and gradually. If she lifts a hind foot threateningly, bump her belly immediately with your knee so that it seems almost as if she's bumping herself. If she threatens to bite, flap your elbow and let her muzzle "run into" it. Don't be aggressive or angry; simply make the wrong behavior uncomfortable in a matter-of-fact way. And be sure to praise her lavishly whenever she does stand quietly. If you're consistent with these strategies, she'll overcome her cinchiness in time.

–Clinton

LESSON NINE

9 Crossing Water

INSTEAD OF FIGHTING WITH YOUR HORSE, USE CONSTANT MOVEMENT AND AN "APPROACH-AND-RETREAT" MENTALITY TO HELP HIM OVERCOME HIS FEAR OF WATER.

Don't just "kick and go" to get your reluctant horse through water. Instead, use circular movement, an "approach-and-retreat" mentality, and rolling back—as I am here—to activate his thinking brain and bolster his courage.

NINE | Crossing Water

IN THIS LESSON, I'M GOING TO TEACH YOU HOW to use my signature approach to help your trail horse overcome his fear of crossing water. As with all the lessons in this series, my strategy will involve moving your horse's feet in various directions to activate the thinking—rather than reacting—side of his brain. This enables him to remain calm, to focus on you, and to realize that what you're asking him to do won't hurt him.

I'll describe how to use circling and rollbacks in front of the stream or pool to gradually bring your horse closer to the water, and eventually move him through it. For areas where circling isn't possible, I'll give you a straightforward approach-and-retreat method that works almost as well.

Both methods work because they reassure your horse that you're not trying to drown him. They encourage him to move only gradually into the water, while allowing retreats onto dry land. You wouldn't teach a child to swim by taking him straight into deep water; you'd start in the shallow end and work gradually toward the deep end, so the child always feels safe. Even though the water you're asking your horse to cross is shallow, he doesn't know that, and the principle is the same: Work gradually until confidence is established.

> **TO GET THE MOST FROM THIS LESSON:**
>
> ■ Make your request sensible by selecting a shallow bit of water (with safe footing) that covers a natural trail or obvious path. From your horse's perspective, it makes more sense to go through water that's blocking his path, than to enter a puddle for no apparent reason.
> ■ If you ride with a group (no more than three or four in total—any more is too distracting), make sure the other horses are calm and confident crossing water. Your horse will likely follow other horses through shallow water, then you can use my methods to ask your horse to go first.
> ■ Avoid riding on frigid or windy days, which can make your horse too rambunctious.
> ■ Before you head out on the trail or attempt at-home training, "longe for respect" (see Lessons 4 through 6) to take the edge off your horse's freshness, assess how he's feeling, and get him tuned in to *you*.

1. When your horse hesitates in front of a water crossing, keep his feet moving. Ride him in a small circle in front of the water, then change direction, as I am here, each time you come to the water's edge, turning toward the water rather than away from it. My horse had been making a circle to his right; here I'm using my left rein and right leg at the cinch to ask him to roll back to his left. Initially, you may not be able to get your horse even this close to the water as you circle and turn back, but just keep at it, giving your horse's thinking brain time to figure things out.

38 CLINTON ANDERSON TRAINING ON THE TRAIL

2. Eventually, as you continue to circle and change directions, one of your horse's front feet will inadvertently step into the water, as is happening here. At this point, just keep doing the same thing, allowing your horse time to realize the water isn't hurting him.

3. With multiple repetitions, your horse will eventually allow both his front feet to enter the water, which is happening here as my horse and I roll back to our left. Don't be too eager to push your horse on through the water as he inches forward; it's the knowledge that he can retreat to safety—just as the small child goes back to the shallow end—that keeps his courage up. Keep circling and entering/leaving the water until you feel your horse's body relaxing under you, and he starts to focus on you instead of the water.

4. Here my horse is ready to walk right on through the water. His head and neck are relaxed and carried normally; his ears are up but not riveted; and he's looking on down the trail, rather than at the water. Be prepared to take as long as you need (as many as 20 minutes or more) to get your horse to this point before you ask him to walk on through.

NINE Crossing Water

WHEN THERE'S NO ROOM TO CIRCLE

A. If there's no room to circle in front of the water, use a literal approach-and-retreat method. First, gently encourage your horse to approach the water as close as he will without having to be forced. At whatever point that is (your horse may not be as close as mine is here), allow him to lower his head and sniff.

B. Then, before your horse tries to back away on his own, ask him to back, using steady pressure on the reins and light pressure from both heels at the cinch. Continue to approach and retreat, gently encouraging your horse to come a bit closer to the water with each approach.

C. When your horse eventually steps into the water with a front foot, don't push him farther in; continue to "keep the pressure off" by backing away again, as I am here.

D. Eventually, you'll get to this point—your horse will realize he has nothing to fear, and you'll be able to walk him straight through the water. ■

PONY 'BUCKS'

Dear Clinton,

My son's 14-year-old POA mare is a great child's pony except she sometimes bucks slightly. She never does this out on trails, but she does occasionally in the arena, especially when first asked to lope. Should my son just ride her through it and go on (usually he can), or spank her, or what? He's just 10, and I don't want him to lose his confidence.

Bobbi Gray,
Fowler, Colorado

Dear Bobbi,

On the trail, your son's mare is enjoying herself. In the arena, she doesn't want to work. "Bucking" is what a rodeo horse does; I'll assume the mare is kicking out, which is usually what happens in these cases. It's the horse's equivalent of a "rude gesture" to say, "No way—I don't want to." The remedy depends on the rider's ability level. My approach would be to spank the horse once and make her move faster, so she quickly learns kicking out just gets her more work. If your son isn't confident enough to do that, he can try riding the mare onto a small, vigorous circle each time she kicks out, as a disincentive. If he's not comfortable doing that, have a more advanced rider—a small adult, perhaps—work the mare for a while until she's over this behavior. In addition to any of these scenarios, have your son do a lot of ground work with his mare daily. As her respect on the ground increases, she'll be less likely to be disrespectful under saddle.

–Clinton

LESSON TEN

10 Gaining Your Horse's Respect

HOW TO DO IT, AND WHY YOU MUST. AS ADAPTED FROM MY NEW BOOK, *DOWNUNDER HORSEMANSHIP*.

Your horse may be dominant in the pasture, but you must be the leader (opposite) in your relationship.

TEN Gaining Your Horse's Respect

CARRY A BUCKET OF GRAIN INTO A PASTURE, AND WHAT happens? The resident broodmares don't share, do they? The dominant mare gets the grain to herself. She doesn't achieve this by flailing away with her hooves, however. She has a step-by-step system—beginning with pinning her ears and shooting a "look," and ending with biting or kicking only if necessary—to remind the other mares who's boss. Because of the pre-established pecking order, there's a minimum of "discipline" involved. The submissive horses know better than to challenge the lead mare, so she easily gets her way.

So it should be between you and your horse. You must be the dominant one, the one he looks to with respect for his marching orders. You must be the leader that he follows humbly and willingly.

In this adaptation from my new book, I'm going to explain this concept, which is the foundation of my training system. I'll tell you why and how, in dealing with your horse, you should use the same logic that horses use with each other.

By following this method, you'll find that your training becomes more effective, and your horse becomes safer and more fun to be around.

WHY RESPECT?

A respectful horse is a willing horse. When you ask him to move, he does so instantly. When you lead him, he walks next to you like a shadow. When you go into his stall in the morning, he comes to you with ears up. In short, he *wants* to be your partner.

A disrespectful horse pins his ears at you, tries to bite or kick, steps on your foot, pushes you out of his way, or simply ignores your requests. You wouldn't let another human "disrespect" you this way; you certainly shouldn't allow a half-ton animal to do it.

For every horse that's abused by his trainer (and I definitely don't condone that), there are many more horses that are abusing their owners. Many of these owners don't even know they're being abused, which only makes matters worse.

The more your horse realizes you control his movement (left), the more he'll respect you, and consider you to be his leader.

You can't correct a problem you're unaware of.

We all want our horses to like us. But friendship is built on respect. The more you spoil your horse, the less he'll respect you. If you only love him, pat him, and feed him, and never ask him to respond promptly or move out of your personal space, he'll never believe you're equipped to lead him. Eventually, he'll stop appreciating anything you do for him, and begin to believe he's in control. At that point, he won't want to spend time with you, because he'll perceive you as weak.

Moreover, a disrespectful horse simply doesn't "listen." That means he won't look to you for guidance at critical points—such as when you're in a tight situation, or negotiating an obstacle, or riding along a busy road. That compromises your safety—and his.

All this can happen because horses are phenomenal "people trainers." We make the most ridiculous excuses for the things our horses have trained us to do. We'll say, "I can't ride with you because my horse doesn't like your horse." Or, "I can't go on this trail because it crosses a ditch, and my horse spooks at ditches." Or, "I can't leave my horse tied because he gets lonely." Or something equally silly.

Rather than making excuses for your horse, take charge of him and become his leader. He'll like and respect you for it, which will enable the two of you to become a true team. The initial work, however, is all up to you.

FOLLOW THE LEADER

Gaining your horse's respect doesn't mean whacking him for no reason. If you simply start thumping on him with a big stick, you won't have respect—you'll have fear. Rather, you must make him feel comfortable whenever he responds to you properly (and thus respectfully), and uncomfortable whenever he doesn't. In this way, he learns that how he feels is his choice—depending on how he interacts with you.

In my book I describe dozens of activities you can do to help foster respectfulness in your horse. Here, I'll explain some of the key elements of my approach, elements that

EXPANDING THE BULL'S-EYE

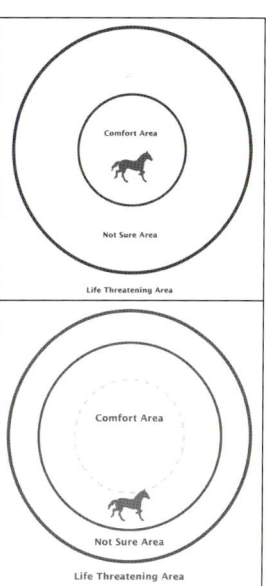

Whenever you try to teach your horse something new, resistance is normal. This is because of your horse's natural desire for safety and comfort.

Imagine a bull's-eye on a target. Your horse is in the middle of this bull's-eye, and surrounding him is his **COMFORT AREA**. He's comfortable and familiar with everything that goes on in that area.

Around the comfort area is his **NOT-SURE AREA**. It's full of anything he doesn't normally do, and your horse would rather avoid going there if possible.

On the outside of that area is what I call the **LIFE-THREATENING AREA**. In this place, your horse thinks he's in serious danger. When your horse finds himself here, the reacting part of his brain takes over. He may kick, buck, bolt, or rear and throw himself backwards—anything to escape what he perceives as a serious threat. This place is home to all the really dangerous things horses can do.

Our goal is to expand our horse's comfort area, so that he's at ease with a wider variety of things. To do that, we have to take him carefully into his not-sure area.

For example, fluttering plastic bags may take your horse out of his comfort area. That means that if you ask him to approach one, he'll resist—because being near the bag puts him into his not-sure area.

At this point, have patience, and as soon as he gives even the slightest "try"— say, a step or two toward the bag—let him come back to his comfort area. (It's important to get at least some small "try" before letting him back into the comfort area; otherwise you're just reinforcing his desire to avoid the not-sure area.)

Keep asking him to enter his not-sure area. Eventually, because he knows you'll keep him safe, he'll be willing to stay there longer and longer.

Every time your horse takes a trip into his not-sure area and leaves it after learning something, his comfort area expands a bit. That means you're on your way to developing a more confident, willing, responsive horse.

CLINTON ANDERSON TRAINING ON THE TRAIL **43**

TEN Gaining Your Horse's Respect

apply in virtually every exercise and training situation. These basic respect-getting strategies include:

MOVE HIS FEET. As I detail in Lessons 1 through 9, this is key. Why? Because it's how horses establish authority over each other.

Think of what happens when that dominant broodmare approaches the bucket of grain. She walks up with ears pinned flat, and the other horses scatter, going forward, backward, left, or right—wherever they need to in order to get out of her way. They do this because the "boss" has said, "move," and she's previously proven to them that she can drive them out of her space whenever she wants to.

When you learn to move your horse in every direction, on the ground and in the saddle, you prove to him that *you're* the boss. Moving his feet also activates the thinking—rather than reacting—side of his brain, which further facilitates training. It enables your horse to remain calm, to focus on you, and to realize that what you're asking of him won't hurt him.

BE CLEAR AND INSISTENT. The more "black and white" you are about what behavior is and is not acceptable, the faster your horse will learn. Shades of gray only confuse him and set him up for failure. "Gray" includes inconsistency (applying cues slightly differently each time you give them), nagging (pick-pick-picking rather than following through and insisting on compliance), and allowing emotion to cloud your judgment (which results in abuse rather than training).

BE IMMEDIATE. For both corrections and rewards, the sooner they occur, the better. The sooner you make your horse feel uncomfortable for unacceptable behavior (instantly backing him up vigorously when he pins his ears at you), the faster he'll connect "uncomfortable" with that behavior, and change it. By the same token, the sooner you make him feel comfortable for the right response (saying "Good boy!" reassuringly when he steps out of your space), the more he'll try to do what you want.

A note about corrections: Make sure your horse's noncompliance is the result of disobedience, and not misunderstand-ing. Never punish him for being confused—it'll only make him fearful.

Also, when a correction is over, it's over. Remember that mare in the pasture—she'll get after a subordinate to keep her from the grain, but then 10 minutes later, the two will be head-to-nose, swishing flies. She doesn't hold a grudge, and neither must you.

USE BODY LANGUAGE. Always be mindful of what you're "saying" to your horse with your posture. Horses communicate primarily via body language, so they're highly attuned to it. Thus, when necessary, you must walk forward assertively and communicate, "Move out of my space!" with your body language (upright posture, muscles tensed). When your horse responds by stepping away, immediately assume a more passive posture (essentially, just relax). You'll be amazed at how quickly he'll understand.

BE ENCOURAGING. Always reward even the slightest try, to let him know when he's on the right track. Do this by removing whatever pressure you've applied, praising with your voice, and/or stroking. You can also use treats, but only as extra reinforcement for a job well done. Treats must always be a bonus, and never a bribe or a payoff. ■

> For information on Clinton's new book, contact the HorseBooksEtc, www.HorseBooksEtc.com or (800) 952-5813

Use assertive body language, as I'm doing here, to let your horse know when his behavior is unacceptable.

44 CLINTON ANDERSON TRAINING ON THE TRAIL